KEEP CALM YOU'RE ONLY 40

D0560173

KEEP CALM
YOU'RE ONLY
40

KEEP CALM

YOU'RE ONLY

40

KEEP CALM YOU'RE ONLY 40

Copyright © Summersdale Publishers Ltd, 2011

With text contributed by Vicky Edwards

All rights reserved.

No part of this book may be reproduced by any means, nor transmitted, nor translated into a machine language, without the written permission of the publishers.

Condition of Sale
This book is sold subject to the condition that it shall not, by way of trade or otherwise, be lent, re-sold, hired out or otherwise circulated in any form of binding or cover other than that in which it is published and without a similar condition including this condition being imposed on the subsequent purchaser.

Summersdale Publishers Ltd
46 West Street
Chichester
West Sussex
PO19 1RP
UK

www.summersdale.com

Printed and bound in the Czech Republic

ISBN: 978-1-84953-222-8

Substantial discounts on bulk quantities of Summersdale books are available to corporations, professional associations and other organisations. For details contact Summersdale Publishers by telephone: +44 (0) 1243 771107, fax: +44 (0) 1243 786300 or email: nicky@summersdale.com.

KEEP CALM

YOU'RE ONLY

40

summersdale

CONTENTS

ANOTHER YEAR OLDER.....6

JUST WHAT I ALWAYS WANTED.....25

GRIN AND BEAR IT.....40

DO A LITTLE DANCE, MAKE A LITTLE LOVE.....59

YOUNG AT HEART.....74

OLDER AND WISER?.....91

LIVE, LOVE AND LAST.....106

ILLS, PILLS AND TWINGES.....121

CHIN UP, CHEST OUT.....138

ANOTHER
YEAR
OLDER

Life begins at 40.

W. B. Pitkin

You're not 40, you're 18 with 22 years' experience.

Anonymous

The lovely thing about being 40 is that you can appreciate 25-year-old men more.

Colleen McCullough

Life begins at 40 – but so do fallen arches, rheumatism, faulty eyesight, and the tendency to tell a story to the same person, three or four times.

Helen Rowland

In dog years,
I'm dead.

Anonymous

The first 40 years of life give us the text; the next 30 supply the commentary on it.

Arthur Schopenhauer

It takes a long time to become young.

Pablo Picasso

I'm 40 and I feel great.
Feel for yourself!

Anonymous

This wine is 40 years old.
It certainly doesn't
show its age.

Cicero

Forty is great – it's the 19th anniversary of your 21st!

Anonymous

We don't understand life any better at 40 than at 20, but we know it and admit it.

Jules Renard

Youth is a circumstance you can't do anything about. The trick is to grow up without getting old.

Frank Lloyd Wright

Forty isn't old, if you're a tree.

Anonymous

Women are most fascinating between the ages of 35 and 40... Since few women ever pass 40, maximum fascination can continue indefinitely.

Christian Dior

As a graduate of the Zsa Zsa Gabor School of Creative Mathematics, I honestly do not know how old I am.

Erma Bombeck

At 20 years of age, the will reigns; at 30, the wit; and at 40, the judgement.

Benjamin Franklin

Women deserve to have more than 12 years between the ages of 28 and 40.

James Thurber

At 15, my mind was bent on learning. At 30, I stood firm. At 40, I had no doubts.

Confucius

JUST WHAT I ALWAYS WANTED

A hug is the perfect gift; one size fits all, and nobody minds if you exchange it.

Anonymous

Why is a birthday cake the only food you can blow on and spit on and everybody rushes to get a piece?

Bobby Kelton

For my 40th I asked her for a dirty weekend. She gave me a trip to the British Bog Snorkelling Championships.

Anonymous

A wise lover values not so much the gift of the lover as the love of the giver.

Thomas à Kempis

The Lord loveth a cheerful giver. He also accepteth from a grouch.

Catherine Hall

Youth is the gift of nature, but age is a work of art.

Garson Kanin

A true friend remembers your birthday but not your age.

Anonymous

I do wish I could tell you my age but it's impossible. It keeps changing all the time.

Greer Garson

Birthdays are nature's way of telling us to eat more cake.

Anonymous

Birthdays are good for you. Statistics show that the people who have the most live the longest.

Larry Lorenzoni

The best birthdays are all those that haven't arrived yet.

Robert Orben

I have everything I had 20 years ago, only it's all a little bit lower.

Gypsy Rose Lee

We know we're getting old when the only thing we want for our birthday is not to be reminded of it.

Anonymous

When it comes to staying young, a mind-lift beats a facelift any day.

Marty Bucella

GRIN
AND
BEAR
IT

Getting old is a bit like getting drunk; everyone else looks brilliant.

Billy Connolly

Like many women my age, I am 28 years old.

Mary Schmich

We turn not older with years, but newer every day.

Emily Dickinson

Age is an issue of mind over matter. If you don't mind, it doesn't matter.

Mark Twain

I knew I was going bald when it was taking me longer and longer to wash my face.

Harry Hill

When I passed 40 I dropped pretence, 'cause men like women who got some sense.

Maya Angelou

‘Age’ is the acceptance of a term of years. But maturity is the glory of years.

Martha Graham

I believe in loyalty; I think when a woman reaches a certain age she likes she should stick to it.

Eva Gabor

You can't turn back the clock. But you can wind it up again.

Bonnie Prudden

Age is something that doesn't matter, unless you are a cheese.

Billie Burke

You can't help getting older, but you don't have to get old.

George Burns

I want to live to be 80 so I can piss more people off.

Charles Bukowski

Youth is a wonderful thing.
What a crime to waste it
on children.

George Bernard Shaw

Time has a wonderful way of weeding out the trivial.

Richard Ben Sapir

Pushing 40? She's hanging on for dear life.

Ivy Compton-Burnett

Ageing is not 'lost youth' but a new stage of opportunity and strength.

Betty Friedan

When it comes to age
we're all in the same boat,
only some of us have been
aboard a little longer.

Leo Probst

The longer I live the more beautiful life becomes.

Frank Lloyd Wright

DO
A LITTLE
DANCE
MAKE
A LITTLE
LOVE

I'll keep swivelling my hips until they need replacing.

Tom Jones

There's a kind of confidence that comes when you're in your forties and fifties, and men find that incredibly attractive.

Peggy Northrop

I must be careful not to get trapped in the past. That's why I tend to forget my songs.

Mick Jagger

The older one grows, the more one likes indecency.

Virginia Woolf

A man is only as old as the woman he feels.

Groucho Marx

I am not old but
mellow like good wine.

Stephen Phillips

The only form of exercise I take is massage.

Truman Capote

When our vices desert us, we flatter ourselves that we are deserting our vices.

François de La Rochefoucauld

It's sex, not youth, that's wasted on the young.

Janet Harris

I'm limitless as far as age is concerned… as long as he has a driver's licence.

Kim Cattrall on dating younger men

If you think hitting 40 is liberating, wait till you hit 50.

Michelle Pfeiffer

The answer to old age is to keep one's mind busy and to go on with one's life as if it were interminable.

Leon Edel

When choosing between two evils, I always like to try the one I've never tried before.

Mae West

I am getting to an age when I can only enjoy the last sport left. It is called hunting for your spectacles.

Edward Grey

YOUNG AT HEART

Men chase golf balls when they're too old to chase anything else.

Groucho Marx

I'd rather be dead than singing 'Satisfaction' when I'm 45.

Mick Jagger

I'll grow old physically, but I won't grow old musically.

Cliff Richard

I have the body of an 18-year-old. I keep it in the fridge.

Spike Milligan

The best years of a woman's life – the ten years between 39 and 40.

Anonymous

We're not the men our fathers were. If we were we would be terribly old.

Flann O'Brien

You know you are getting older when 'happy hour' is a nap.

Gray Kristofferson

The older I get, the older old is.

Tom Baker

Granny said she was going to grow old gracefully, but she left it too late.

Christine Kelly

By the time I have money to burn, my fire will have burnt out.

Anonymous

If you obey all the rules, you miss all the fun.

Katharine Hepburn

The older a man gets, the farther he had to walk to school as a boy.

Henry Brightman

Some kids in Italy call me 'Mama Jazz'; I thought that was so cute. As long as they don't call me 'Grandma Jazz'.

Ella Fitzgerald

Sometimes when a man recalls the good old days, he's really thinking of his bad young days.

Anonymous

I don't plan to grow old gracefully; I plan to have facelifts until my ears meet.

Rita Rudner

You'll find as you grow older that you weren't born such a great while ago after all. The time shortens up.

Frank Lloyd Wright

OLDER AND WISER?

Keep true to the dreams of thy youth.

Friedrich von Schiller

Yes, time flies. And where did it leave you? Old too soon… smart too late.

Mike Tyson

None are so old
as those who have
outlived enthusiasm.

Henry David Thoreau

You're only as young as the last time you changed your mind.

Timothy Leary

Old age is like a plane flying through a storm. Once you are aboard there is nothing you can do.

Golda Meir

If you want a thing done well, get a couple of old broads to do it.

Bette Davis

A prune is an experienced plum.

John Trattner

Be wise with speed; a fool at 40 is a fool indeed.

Edward Young

From 40 to 50 a man must move upward, or the natural falling off in the vigour of life will carry him rapidly downward.

Oliver Wendell Holmes Jr

A man is not old as long as he is seeking something.

Jean Rostand

Wisdom doesn't necessarily come with age. Sometimes age just shows up all by itself.

Tom Wilson

If I had to live my life over again, I'd be a plumber.

Albert Einstein

Cherish all your happy moments: they make a fine cushion for old age.

Christopher Morley

As we grow older, our bodies get shorter and our anecdotes longer.

Robert Quillen

LIVE
LOVE
AND
LAST

To stop ageing,
keep on raging.

Michael Forbes

Everyone is the age of their heart.

Guatemalan proverb

One should never make one's debut in a scandal. One should reserve that to give interest to one's old age.

Oscar Wilde

At middle age the soul should be opening up like a rose, not closing up like a cabbage.

John Andrew Holmes

Age is whatever you think it is. You are as old as you think you are.

Muhammad Ali

He who laughs, lasts!

Mary Pettibone Poole

No matter how old you are, there's always something good to look forward to.

Lynn Johnston

At age 20, we worry about what others think of us. At 40, we don't care what they think of us.

Ann Landers

Age does not protect you from love. But love to some extent, protects you from age.

Jeanne Moreau

Don't let ageing get you down. It's too hard to get back up.

John Wagner

Tomorrow's gone –
we'll have tonight!

Dorothy Parker

There are three stages of a man's life: he believes in Santa Claus, he doesn't believe in Santa Claus, he is Santa Claus.

Anonymous

It's a good idea to obey all the rules when you're young just so you'll have the strength to break them when you're old.

Mark Twain

Regular naps prevent old age, especially if you take them while driving.

Anonymous

ILLS PILLS AND TWINGES

My doctor told me to do something that puts me out of breath, so I've taken up smoking again.

Jo Brand

My mother is no spring chicken although she has got as many chemicals in her as one.

Dame Edna Everage

I don’t want a flu jab. I like getting flu. It gives me something else to complain about.

David Letterman

I keep fit. Every morning I do a hundred laps of an Olympic-sized swimming pool in a small motor launch.

Peter Cook

Middle age is when you choose your cereal for the fibre, not the toy.

Anonymous

Some grow bitter with age; the more their teeth drop out, the more biting they get.

George D. Prentice

I'd like to learn to ski but I'm worried about my knees. They creak... and I'm afraid they might start an avalanche.

Jonathan Ross

Age seldom arrives smoothly or quickly. It's more often a succession of jerks.

Jean Rhys

Nothing is more responsible for the good old days than a bad memory.

Franklin Pierce Adams

I go slower as time goes faster.

Mason Cooley

What most persons consider as virtue, after the age of 40 is simply a loss of energy.

Voltaire

I hope to have it replaced very soon.

Terry Wogan on people saying that he didn't know the meaning of 'hip'

Life is a moderately good play with a badly written third act.

Truman Capote

I don't know how you feel about old age... but in my case I didn't even see it coming. It hit me from the rear.

Phyllis Diller

The older you get, the more you tell it like it used to be.

Anonymous

Old minds are like old horses; you must exercise them if you wish to keep them in working order.

John Quincy Adams

CHIN UP CHEST OUT

Inflation is when you pay 15 dollars for the 10-dollar haircut you used to get for five dollars when you had hair.

Sam Ewing

Wrinkles are hereditary. Parents get them from their children.

Doris Day

She may very well pass for 43 in the dusk with the light behind her!

W. S. Gilbert

Grey hair is
God's graffiti.

Bill Cosby

A woman past 40 should make up her mind to be young, and not her face.

Billie Burke

As the arteries grow hard,
the heart grows soft.

H. L. Mencken

As we grow old… the beauty steals inward.

Ralph Waldo Emerson

I'm not denying my age, I'm embellishing my youth.

Tamara Reynolds

I guess I don't so much mind being old, as I mind being fat and old.

Peter Gabriel

The secret of staying young is to live honestly, eat slowly and lie about your age.

Lucille Ball

If you want to look young and thin, hang around old fat people.

Jim Eason

The easiest way to diminish the appearance of wrinkles is to keep your glasses off when you look in the mirror.

Joan Rivers

Professionally,
I have no age.

Kathleen Turner

You know you're getting old when you can pinch an inch on your forehead.

John Mendoza

Thirty-five is when you finally get your head together and your body starts falling apart.

Caryn Leschen

As you get older, the pickings get slimmer, but the people don't.

Carrie Fisher

People say that age is just a state of mind. I say it's more about the state of your body.

Geoffrey Parfitt

Women are not forgiven for ageing. Robert Redford's lines of distinction are my old-age wrinkles.

Jane Fonda

Wrinkles should merely indicate where smiles have been.

Mark Twain

KEEP
CALM
AND
DRINK
UP